KU-307-551

Shakespeare
and the
Theatre

Jane Shuter

Raintree

Raintree is an imprint of Capstone Global Library Limited, a company incorporated in England and Wales having its registered office at 7 Pilgrim Street, London, EC4V 6LB – Registered company number: 6695582

www.raintreepublishers.co.uk
myorders@raintreepublishers.co.uk

Text © Capstone Global Library Limited 2014
First published in hardback in 2014
Paperback edition first published in 2015
The moral rights of the proprietor have been asserted.

All rights reserved. No part of this publication may be reproduced in any form or by any means (including photocopying or storing it in any medium by electronic means and whether or not transiently or incidentally to some other use of this publication) without the written permission of the copyright owner, except in accordance with the provisions of the Copyright, Designs and Patents Act 1988 or under the terms of a licence issued by the Copyright Licensing Agency, Saffron House, 6–10 Kirby Street, London EC1N 8TS (www.cla.co.uk). Applications for the copyright owner's written permission should be addressed to the publisher.

Edited by Andrew Farrow and Abby Colich
Designed by Steve Mead
Original illustrations © Capstone Global Library Ltd 2014
Illustrated by HL Studios
Picture research by Elizabeth Alexander
Production by Victoria Fitzgerald
Originated by Capstone Global Library Ltd
Printed and bound in China by Leo Paper Group

ISBN 978 1 406 27332 8 (hardback)
17 16 15 14 13
10 9 8 7 6 5 4 3 2 1

British Library Cataloguing in Publication Data
Shuter, Jane
Shakespeare and the Theatre. – (Shakespeare Alive)
A full catalogue record for this book is available from the British Library.

Acknowledgements
We would like to thank the following for permission to reproduce photographs: Alamy: pp. 7 (© The Bridgeman Art Library Ltd), 8 (© Greg Balfour Evans); 17 (© Hilary Morgan), 50 (© Felipe Trueba); American Shakespeare Center's production of Much Ado About Nothing featuring Aiden O'Reilly, Gregory Jon Phelps and Chris Johnston: p. 33 (Photo by Tommy Thompson, 2012); The Bridgeman Art Library: pp. 18 (Private Collection), 35 (© Dulwich Picture Gallery, London, UK), 37 (© Dulwich Picture Gallery, London, UK), 41 (© Dulwich Picture Gallery, London, UK), 44 (Haags Gemeentemuseum, The Hague, Netherlands); © David Cooper. With kind permission of the Governors of Dulwich College. Dulwich College MS 19: p. 52; THE KOBAL COLLECTION / SPARHAM, LAURIE: p. 47 (MIRAMAX FILMS/ UNIVERSAL PICTURES); Reproduced by permission of the Marquess of Bath, Longleat House, Warminster, Wiltshire, Great Britain: p. 54; Shakespeare's Globe: pp. 21 (photograph by Andy Bradshaw, 2008), 22 (photograph by Pete Le May), 27, 31 (CGI by Allies and Morrison), 39 (photograph by John Tramper, 2012), 49 (photograph by John Tramper, 2006), 56 (photograph by Pete Le May); Shutterstock: pp. 24-25 (© Natutik); TopFoto.co.uk: pp. 13 (TopFoto.co.uk), 14 (TopFoto.co.uk), 55 top (Johan Persson / ArenaPAL), 55 bottom (Johan Persson / ArenaPAL); Utrecht, University Library, Ms. 842, fol. 132r: p. 29.

Design features: Shutterstock: (© R-studio), (© Tribalium), (© tkada).

Cover photograph of Othello at Shakespeare's Globe Theatre, London, Great Britain May 11, 2007, reproduced with permission from TopFoto. co.uk (Elliott Franks / ArenaPAL).

We would like to thank Farah Karim-Cooper for her invaluable help in the preparation of this book.

Every effort has been made to contact copyright holders of material reproduced in this book. Any omissions will be rectified in subsequent printings if notice is given to the publisher.

GREENWICH LIBRARIES

CO

3 8028 02155214 3	
Askews & Holts	06-Aug-2014
T822.33 BLUE	£15.99
4380131	

Contents

Some words are shown in bold, **like this**. You can find out what they mean by looking in the glossary.

Shakespeare's England

William Shakespeare is famous for his plays, written from about 1590 to 1614. He was born in Stratford-upon-Avon, Warwickshire, but worked mainly in London where the newly set-up theatres were. This book looks at the world of the theatre in his time. However, to understand Shakespeare and his work we need to understand the world he lived in. Society in England in Shakespeare's time was very different from modern society. One big difference is that most people believed strongly in the idea of a social order.

What was the "social order"?

The social order was a pyramid of wealth and power with a ruler at the top and very poor people at the bottom. Everyone knew his or her place in the social order, and the **rights** and **duties** of that place. Everything about them, from their work to how they dressed and what they ate, reflected their place. England's king or queen had the right to be obeyed by everyone in the country. The ruler's duty was to run the country well. An **apprentice** who was learning a trade had a duty to obey his master. His master had a duty to teach the apprentice a trade, house him, and provide his food and clothes.

KINGS/QUEENS
LORDS/NOBLES
KNIGHTS/GENTLEMEN

Above this line, people were allowed to carry a sword and have a coat of arms.

CITIZENS AND BURGESSES
important and rich townspeople often involved in local government

MERCHANTS, SKILLED CRAFTSMEN, YEOMEN
(who owned their farms)
Most were well off, some were rich

Below this line, people owned no land or houses.

SHOPKEEPERS, TRADERS, CRAFTSMEN, TENANT FARMERS
(who rented their farms)
most lived comfortably, some were well off

THE POOR
the best-off worked, e.g, servants, labourers, miners. The worst-off had no work so they begged

This diagram shows the social order in Shakespeare's time. In 1596, Shakespeare applied for a coat of arms for his father, moving him from citizen and **burgess** to the rank of **gentleman**.

Shakespeare's father was a craftsman, and the most usual work for the sons of craftsmen was to follow their fathers in the same trade or become apprenticed to another craftsman.

The countryside

In Shakespeare's time, about 75 per cent of people lived in the countryside, in villages, or in small towns. Most people worked in farming. Because the wool trade made a lot of money, many farmers had changed from farming crops to keeping sheep for wool. Many farmworkers lost their jobs, and the homes that went with them, and had to look for work elsewhere. But there was not much work. This situation was made worse by the growing population. For the first time in living memory, it was possible to be out of work not because you didn't want a job, but because there were no jobs. People moved around looking for work. Shakespeare was one of many who left his family home to work somewhere else.

The **nobility** and **gentry** had homes and land in the countryside, even if they also had a house in a large town. Land showed how well off you were. People who made money bought land; it made you someone to look up to. Shakespeare bought land when he could afford it, as did many of the people he worked with.

I was there...

Grain, not sheep

In 1597, the government passed a law in favour of the growing of crops rather than keeping sheep for wool. Robert Cecil, Queen Elizabeth I's most important adviser, made notes about the reasons for the law. Here is a modernized extract:

A few people getting richer, the rest poorer. If people farm crops it will reduce unemployment, drunkenness and vice. It will reduce the swarms of poor, unemployed, wandering people that are a misery to themselves and a danger to the government. It will save the government from having to rely on buying grain from other countries.

A rising population

The population in Shakespeare's time was rising steadily. This rising population had several effects:

- There were more people needing work at a time when unemployment was rising anyway.
- There was less food to go round, so food prices rose.
- People who could not find work in the countryside moved to the towns, hoping to find work there.

You can find more information about wages, incomes, and the price of goods on page 60.

Growing towns and cities

Towns and city grew enormously. London grew most rapidly. As the biggest city in England, it had a population of about 120,000 in 1550. By 1600, its population was 200,000, and by 1650, it was 400,000. The next most important cities were: Norwich, Bristol, and York. In about 1520, their approximate populations were Norwich 12,000, Bristol 10,000, and York 8,000. By 1603, they had grown to 15,000, 12,000, and 11,000. Towns were centres of government and trade. As towns grew, so did the variety of shops, **inns**, and entertainment they provided. By the 1570s, this included theatres in London. The more opportunities a city provided the more people were drawn there.

SHAKESPEARE'S EXPERIENCE

The food crisis

When Shakespeare was working in London in the 1590s, there was a food crisis in England. There was a run of bad harvests, causing a severe shortage of the grain which was used to make both bread and beer, basic foods for the poor. People went hungry and some starved, especially in towns and cities. Many more were so weak that they were more likely to catch infectious illnesses.

GREENWICH LIBRARIES

3 8028 02155214 3

What was London like?

London was one of the biggest cities in Europe and was home to the very wealthy, the very poor, and all levels of the social order in between. It was in two parts: the City (inside the city walls) and the suburbs that grew up outside those walls. People moved to London from all over England, and also from other countries. A large number were Dutch, but there were also significant numbers of French, Italians, Spaniards, and Scots. London's rapidly expanding suburbs spread all around the city walls and south of the River Thames.

Keeping people entertained

London attracted a large number of tourists. It offered a vast range of entertainment for everyone in the city, residents and tourists. People could play tennis and bowls, watch bear-**baiting**, bull-baiting, and **cockfighting**, or gamble and watch actors perform plays.

This painting from 1570 shows a feast in Bermondsey, on the south bank of the Thames. At the time it was a village, with the road leading to the river. You can just see the Tower of London on the other side of the river through the gap in the two trees on the left. By the time Shakespeare died (1616), Bermondsey was part of London.

Where did actors perform?

By the time Shakespeare arrived in London, at some point in the late 1580s, theatres were a feature of London life. Bristol is the only other city where there is known to have been a purpose-built theatre (on Wine Street, 1604–1625). Before theatres, groups of actors travelled the country, performing in the courtyards of inns, on temporary stages in market squares, or in **guildhalls** and other large rooms. Most were genuine actors. Others were little more than bands of thieves who used performances to draw a crowd so they could pick pockets or rob empty homes.

Some **noblemen** employed groups of entertainers as part of their **households**, to act short plays, sing and dance. These groups were named after their employers, for example, the Earl of Leicester's Men. These entertainers also travelled if their lord didn't need them. Some entertained other nobles and invited guests, or even performed at **court**). Many nobles' **companies** also performed in public. The Earl of Leicester's Men **played** regularly at the Cross Keys Inn, London, as well as at court.

The George Inn, Southwark, was built in 1676, but has a similar design as older courtyard inns. It shows how people could have watched from the galleries that ran around the sides of the courtyard, as well as standing in the yard itself, but inns in Shakespeare's time usually only had one gallery level, not two.

SHAKESPEARE'S EXPERIENCE

The City of London

London, like all English cities and some towns in Shakespeare's time, had its own local government. A Lord Mayor and 12 Aldermen ran the City, while following government laws. The City administration saw acting companies as a disruption and regularly banned them from performing in the City. These bans did not apply to "**liberties**" inside the City. These areas once belonged to monasteries and were not under City law. Church lands were governed by church laws. When the lands were taken from the monasteries they were allowed to stay outside the control of City **officials**.

Acting companies also travelled around the country – they played in Stratford in 1573, 1576–1577, and 1586–1587. All through Shakespeare's time in London, touring was part of an acting company's life.

Government control

In 1559, Elizabeth I issued a **proclamation** that all acting companies had to have a licence from a nobleman. In 1572, a new government law ("An Act for the Punishment of Vagabonds and for the Relief of the Poor") said actors who didn't have a **licence** from a nobleman would be punished as **vagrants**.

Why build theatres?

The popularity of plays encouraged some London businessmen to build theatres to make money. It was easier to draw large crowds and charge for entertainment in London. Most of them seem to **lease** land for a set number of years, and then build a theatre or convert an existing building. Then they rented the theatre to an acting company, usually for two to three years. All sorts of things could go wrong with a system this complex. Legal documents that survive from the time show that they sometimes did. By the time Shakespeare arrived, there were three established theatres, and the demand for plays was high. Touring companies kept moving on, so only needed a few plays. Audiences visiting a permanent theatre wanted new plays, not the same plays over and over again.

The first theatres

The first theatre, the Red Lion, was built in 1567 by John Brayne. He converted the Red Lion Inn, in Stepney, outside the City. There is little evidence of how successful it was. However, the demand was there because three more outdoor and two **indoor theatres** were opened between 1575 and 1577.

In 1576, Brayne and James Burbage leased some land and built the Theatre, just outside the city walls. Burbage was the leading actor with the Earl of Leicester's Men, the company that played in the Theatre for its first two years. Within two years, the Curtain was built nearby. Newington Butts was built further outside the city in 1576. Inn yard productions continued, and there were more after the first theatres were built.

Types of theatre

There were two kinds of theatre: indoor theatres and outdoor theatres. Indoor theatres developed out of private performances in the homes of the nobility, halls, schools, universities, or the Inns of Court, where law was taught. A temporary stage was put up in a suitable room and seats arranged on three sides. The first purpose-built indoor theatre (Paul's) was built in 1575 and the second (Blackfriars) in 1576. Indoor theatres were smaller than outdoor theatres, and prices were higher. Until 1609, when Shakespeare's company started to use the Blackfriars indoor theatre, only boy companies played in indoor theatres.

Outdoor theatres developed from the courtyard inns and the **arenas** built for animal baiting. They had a central yard (square or many-sided) which was open to the sky. They had galleries on three sides, usually two stories high. Outdoor theatres held more people than indoor ones, but many members of the audience had to stand in the yard – the open space around the stage. Outdoor theatre companies were men and boys.

WHAT NOW?

The modern Globe is on the south side of the River Thames, close to the site of the Globe in Shakespeare's time. The builders used all the information available at the time about outdoor theatres, more so than any previous attempt to build an outdoor theatre. This book will refer to the modern Globe, and use several images of it, because they give us the best possible idea of what an outdoor theatre was like.

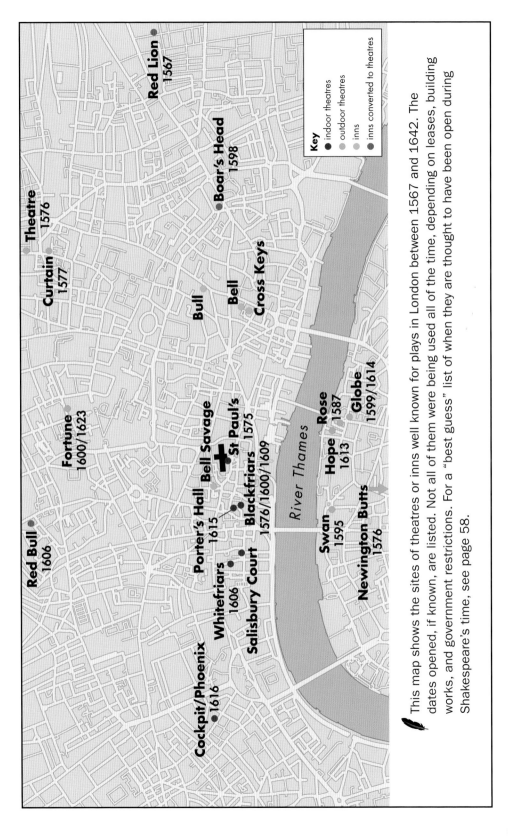

This map shows the sites of theatres or inns well known for plays in London between 1567 and 1642. The dates opened, if known, are listed. Not all of them were being used all of the time, depending on leases, building works, and government restrictions. For a "best guess" list of when they are thought to have been open during Shakespeare's time, see page 58.

Red Lion
1567

Theatre
1576

Curtain
1577

Boar's Head
1598

Bull

Bell

Cross Keys

Fortune
1600/1623

Bell Savage

St Paul's
1575

Blackfriars
1576/1600/1609

Porter's Hall
1615

Red Bull
1606

Whitefriars
1606

Salisbury Court

Cockpit/Phoenix
1616

River Thames

Rose
1587

Globe
1599/1614

Hope
1613

Swan
1595

Newington Butts
1576

Key
● indoor theatres
● outdoor theatres
● inns
● inns converted to theatres

Who went to the theatre?

Plays were very popular, but not everyone had to go to a theatre or inn to see one. Elizabeth I and James I both enjoyed plays, but they sent for acting companies to come to court to perform. But, other than royalty, people from all levels of the social order went to theatres, in the afternoon.

Different audiences?

Different theatres attracted different audiences. Indoor theatres were only really for the well-off. The cheapest seats were 6d – six times as much as standing in the yard of an outdoor theatre. Nobles and other important people were most likely to go to an outdoor theatre on a day the indoor theatres were closed. Most working people had to go to an outdoor theatre and stand if they wanted to see a play. The 1d admission was all they could afford.

I was there...

Ambassador at a play

This extract is from the letters of an Italian, Antonio Galli, describing the visit of Antonio Foscarini, the Venetian ambassador, to a play in 1613. Foscarini was fond of plays and is known to have gone to the Fortune theatre, too.

He went the other day to a playhouse called the Curtain, which is out beyond his house. It is an **infamous** place. No good citizen or gentleman would show his face there. And what was worse, he wanted to avoid paying for a little room, not even sitting among the better sort. He insisted on standing in the yard, among the gang of porters and carters. He gave as his excuse that he was hard of hearing – as if he could have understood the language anyway!

op sulcken .laren word Het goet tot
London over Straet gebracht?

Een Porterofte
Arbeyder van Lon

Michael van Meer, from Antwerp, visited London in about 1614. He kept a record of his visit, complete with pictures he drew. This one shows a carter and a market porter at work on the streets of London. They would have gone to stand in the yard of an outdoor theatre, like the Red Bull. It had a reputation for putting on plays likely to appeal most to such an audience.

Making a choice

The nobility and gentry could afford to go to indoor and outdoor theatres, as could London's wealthier citizens. So how did they choose? People who could afford to go to either type of theatre might make their choice based on the play being performed, the actors taking part, or the weather.

Indoor theatres were sheltered from the weather, but it was perfectly possible to be both sheltered and comfortable in an outdoor theatre. It was also possible to avoid mixing with the poorer theatre-goers. Outdoor theatres did have more expensive gallery seats. They also had lords' rooms over the stage for the most important members of the audience. Sometimes a noble would take all these seats for a play. In 1607, the ambassador sent from Venice to London did this for a performance of Shakespeare's *Pericles*.

How did they get there?

There were theatres north and south of the River Thames (see the map on page 11). Poorer people walked to the theatre. Many people went on horseback. Coaches, a fairly recent invention, were only for the well-off. People who lived near indoor theatres complained about all the coaches before and after performances. People who wanted to cross the river had to use the only bridge, London Bridge, or take a wherry, a small boat used like a water taxi. The theatres brought the wherrymen a good **income**. When the theatres were closed, for example because of outbreaks of **plague**, they often sent **petitions** to the government to open the theatres again because of their loss of income.

This painting by Michael van Meer shows well-off people being rowed across the Thames, with London Bridge in the background.

A different experience

Audiences in Shakespeare's time went to hear a play, as much as see it – the word "audience" comes from the Latin for "to hear". This doesn't mean they didn't want to watch, too – the word "spectator" comes from the Latin word "to watch" and was used about audiences at the time. Some of them also went to be seen. That is why the lords' rooms in an outdoor theatre were above and behind the stage, facing the audience. People sitting there came in by a back door and didn't have to rub shoulders with the rest of the audience. They sat apart, able to hear well, and in comfort, possibly with small tiled stoves for warmth. The rest of the audience could see how lucky and how well-dressed they were.

How did they behave?

Audiences didn't sit quietly during a performance. They hissed at the villains, cheered for the heroes, and shouted out remarks. They offered advice if a **character** asked a question. They stamped their feet, banged the boards, and clapped. They ate, drank, and smoked tobacco if they could afford the three pennies for a small pipeful. They went in and out of the theatre – to buy food and to stretch their legs. There were no intervals in outdoor theatre performances and no toilets. Occasionally, they even got into fights with each other.

Bad behaviour went on at all social levels. Apprentices and servants scuffled in the yards of outdoor theatres. In 1632, two nobles had a fight in the Blackfriars theatre over who should have the key and the sole use of the best box.

Actors must have been used to audiences behaving badly. Even so, there are a few examples of actors losing their tempers with members of the audience. In the Theatre, in 1590, Richard Burbage went up to a man, grabbed him by the nose, and threatened to beat him up if he didn't behave.

WHAT NOW?

Modern audiences

Modern audiences at Shakespeare's Globe get to eat and drink in the theatre, and they talk to each other, quietly, too. They go in and out during the performances, although there is an interval. They join in and shout if the actors encourage them to, but not otherwise. They don't usually get into fights.

Modern audiences do create problems that were unknown in Shakespeare's time – just because they want to use gadgets that were not invented in Shakespeare's time. So they have to be warned not to take film or photos during the performance and not to use mobile phones. When it rains, the audience in the yard have to be asked not to put up umbrellas!

There are also more facilities for modern audiences. There are toilets and a shop that sells souvenirs. The seats in the theatre are numbered. So each audience member who is sitting down has a seat number on their ticket that matches a number of painted on the benches. They have more space each than audience members would have had in Shakespeare's time.

Opposition to theatres

The theatres were not popular with everyone. If you believed what was said by those who were against the theatres, you would think they overflowed with people not there for the plays, but to cut purses and sell stolen goods. The City authorities thought theatres were a nuisance. Religious groups complained about them, too, especially when they performed on Sundays, or during Lent or church services. Individual people also objected. All these groups sent a stream of complaints to the government; some published **pamphlets** of their objections. There were several different arguments:

- Theatres draw people away from church services.
- Theatres are morally questionable places.
- Theatres attract thieves and con men.
- The crowds spread infectious diseases (especially the plague).
- The crowds are noisy.
- The crowds fight and might start riots.
- The crowds clog the streets with their horses or carriages.

I was there...

Plays or sermons?

This extract is a modernized version of a letter to Frances Walsingham, one of Queen Elizabeth's advisers, written in 1587. The writer was complaining of how the theatres drew people away from church services.

Every day in the week the players' bills [posters] are set up around the city, some in the name of her Majesty's Men, some of the Earl of Leicester, some of the Earl of Oxford, the Lord Admiral's, and others. So that when the bells call for the sermon the trumpets sound for the stages – woe is me! The playhouses are pestered and the churches are naked. At one, it isn't possible to get a place, at the other there are plenty of empty seats.

Bad neighbours?

In 1609, people who lived near Blackfriars were outraged at plans to change its use. They had been used to the weekly performances by boy actors. Now they had adult actors, from the Globe, playing almost daily all through the winter. They complained about the noise, the crowds, the coach jams, and the fact the actors performed at the same time as church services.

I was there...

Anti-theatre petition

This extract is from a petition to the government by local residents to stop performances at the Blackfriars, written in 1619. Hackney coaches were hired coaches, rather than coaches owned by the nobility.

There is daily such a number of people and such a multitude of coaches (many of them Hackney coaches, bringing up all sorts) that sometimes all our streets cannot contain them... The inhabitants cannot reach their houses or have goods delivered.

Marion Frith was a woman who became notorious in 1611 for dressing and behaving in public like a man. Middleton and Dekker wrote a play about her called *Moll Cutpurse* that sensationalized her activities. Frith herself came, in male dress, to performances and sat on the stage, making herself very obvious. This was the sort of behaviour that critics said the theatres encouraged.

Not always open

Legal disputes, the ending of leases, building works, government restrictions, and not making enough money could all force a theatre to close. There were several long-term closures of the theatres, and other places where crowds gathered, such as baiting arenas, because of plague. When this happened, acting companies went on tour, but some did not survive long closures.

SHAKESPEARE'S EXPERIENCE

Plague

The plague was a deadly disease. It came in two forms: bubonic (mostly in summer, spread by the fleas on rats) and pneumonic (mostly in winter, spread by sneezing and coughing). It broke out fairly regularly in Shakespeare's time, especially in London with its crowds and poor sanitation. The government closed theatres when the numbers of dead reached a certain level (which varied). When Shakespeare was in London there were four especially bad outbreaks, leading to almost year-long closures of the theatres.

A Rod for Run-awayes.

Gods Tokens.

Of his fearefull Iudgements, sundry wayes pronounced vpon this City, and on feuerall perfons, both flying from it, and ftaying in it.

Expreffed in many dreadfull Examples of fudden Death, falne vpon both young and old, within this City, and the Suburbes, in the Fields, and open Streets, to the terrour of all thofe who liue, and to the warning of thofe who are to dye, to be ready when God Almighty fhall bee pleafed to call them.

By Tho. Dekker.

Lord, haue mercy on London.
I follow. We fly.
Wee dye. Keepe out.

This illustration from a 1625 pamphlet about the plague sums up the fear at the time about the disease, and the feeling that it was sent as a punishment from God.

I was there...

Rampage at the Cockpit

This modernized extract is from a description of the destruction of the Cockpit on 4 March 1617.

> Other apprentices made for Drury Lane, where a new playhouse has been built. They surrounded it, broke in, wounded several of the players and broke open their trunks. Whatever clothes, books or other things they found they burnt and cut into pieces. Not content with that, they got on the top of the house and threw the tiles off it. If the JPs [Justices of the Peace, local officials] and sheriff had not raised help, and stopped them, they would have pulled it down to the ground. In this skirmish one apprentice was shot through the head with a pistol.

Destroyed!

Theatres could also be closed by various disasters. In 1580, an earthquake caused damage all over south-east England. The Theatre and the Curtain both had to make repairs. Fire was a real threat to the theatres, and to London generally, where many buildings were wood-framed and thatched. The first Globe, on Bankside, burned down in 1613. The Fortune, in the northern suburbs of the city, burned down in 1621. Both were rebuilt. The fires were accidents. Other destruction was more deliberate.

In 1616, Christopher Beeston leased some land with a cockpit on it, where people watched cocks (male chickens) fight each other for sport. He converted it to an indoor theatre, called the Cockpit. Beeston was a leading actor in the Queen's Men, the acting company at the Red Bull at the time. He clearly intended to move the company from the Red Bull to the Cockpit. This angered local apprentices, who would not be able to afford indoor theatre prices. Apprentices had Shrove Tuesday (a religious holiday) off and traditionally ran wild on that day. The Cockpit was among the buildings they attacked and damaged in 1617.

Outdoor theatres

The size of outdoor theatres varied depending on the land available and how much the person building the theatre could afford. They had a wooden frame on a brick base, with wood and plaster filling the gaps between the timbers. The exception to this style is the second Fortune, which was built of brick.

Shared features

All outdoor theatres had:

- a central yard that was open to the sky
- a raised stage sticking out into the yard
- a roof over the stage, called "the heavens"
- a backstage area where actors dressed and waited to come on
- above the backstage area were lords' rooms, a music room, rooms for storage, and a room level with "the heavens" (above the stage) to work the special effects from
- roofed seating, called galleries, all around the yard, on two or three levels.

I was there...

A tourist's view

In 1599, a Swiss tourist, Thomas Platter, wrote about his visit to London in his diary. He went to the theatre several times.

Daily at two in the afternoon, London has two, sometimes three plays running in different places, competing with each other, and those which play best obtain most spectators. The playhouses are so constructed that they [the actors] play on a raised stage, so that everyone has a good view. There are different galleries where the seating is better and more comfortable and therefore more expensive. Those who stand below only pay one English penny, but if you wish to sit, you enter by another door and pay another penny. If you want to sit in the most comfortable (cushioned) seats where you not only see everything well, but also can be seen, then you pay yet another penny at another door.

What did it cost?

The middle and upper galleries
There may have been some cheaper standing room in these galleries. After this, people sat on benches and prices ranged from 2d to 6d; depending on position and level of comfort (whether a cushion was provided for the bench, for example).

The lords' rooms
These were the most expensive rooms. People had comfortable seating, with cushions. They could hear the play, see some of it, and be seen by the audience. The cost varied from 6d to 1s.

The gentlemen's rooms
These were smallish rooms, sometimes decorated. People sat on stools with cushions and usually paid 6d.

The lower gallery
Sitting on benches in the gallery at ground level cost 2d.

Collecting the money
Both men and women "gatherers" stood at various doors in the theatre and took the money. The busiest gatherers were those on the main door that led into the yard. Then gatherers to take the extra pennies for the seating stood at the place where the admission prices rose. Gatherers at the back door took the money from people going to the lords' rooms and, possibly, the gentlemen's rooms.

The yard
The audience in the yard (known as groundlings) stood, with no shelter. It cost them 1d – the price never changed.

The yard floor

The modern Globe has a concrete yard floor that slopes slightly downwards towards the stage. Outdoor theatres in Shakespeare's time had a similar slope in the yard to drain the rainwater away. They had some kind of paving – an earth floor would have turned to mud if it rained. There is evidence that the Rose had a floor made from a mixture of silt from the river, ash, **clinker**, and hazelnut shells. Other theatres had mortar yard floors.

The roof of the modern Globe is thatched with reeds. The first Globe was thatched, but the second had a tile roof. The roof over the stage is "the heavens". The pillars are wood painted to look like marble, as was done in Shakespeare's time.

Decoration

Visitors to the theatres said the stage and the area at the back of it were beautifully decorated. A visitor to the Swan in 1596 said it had wooden pillars "painted in such excellent imitation of marble that you would believe it is marble indeed". The heavens were also decorated. There is some evidence that the more expensive gentlemen's rooms had colourful wall hangings. The rest of the theatre might have been painted, but there is not enough evidence to be certain.

Moving around

People went to the most expensive seats through a back door of the theatre that took them through the backstage area, so they did not have to mix with the rest of the audience. However, people sitting in the cheaper upper gallery areas needed stairs to reach their benches. Smaller theatres probably had stairs running up from the yard. Bigger theatres probably had stairs before the audience reached the yard, but after they had paid to go in. This split people up and cut down on crowding.

WHAT NOW?

Pricing

The modern Globe has a very different pricing system to the original Globe.

In both cases, standing in the yard has always been cheapest. After that, however, the modern Globe's prices rise depending on how good a view of the stage a seat gives. So the most expensive seats on each level in the modern theatre are the first few rows directly facing the stage.

The lords' rooms are seldom used in the modern theatre, because the view of the stage is poor. You mostly see the actors' backs, because they face the main audience most of the time. In Shakespeare's time, the seats in the lords' rooms were the most expensive seats. They kept the nobility, or whoever else could afford the price of a seat, separate from the rest of the audience. Sitting in the lords' rooms also let them be seen, and they could hear the play as well.

The first Globe theatre

The first Globe was built by the Burbage brothers, because there were problems with their lease on the Theatre, which was due to run out in 1597. Giles Allen (who leased James Burbage the land the Theatre stood on) said he wouldn't renew the lease. In 1596, Burbage bought a large upstairs room in Blackfriars and built an indoor playhouse. The people who lived there strongly objected. Burbage was banned from using the Blackfriars. In February 1597, he died, leaving his sons, Cuthbert and Richard, with a lease soon to run out and an indoor theatre they couldn't use.

Desperate measures

Richard Burbage was the leading actor in the Lord Chamberlain's Men, who used the Theatre. The company (Shakespeare was a member) decided to move to the Curtain. This was good for Richard Burbage as an actor; the company kept playing. It was bad for him and his brother as businessmen. They lost the owner's share of the company's takings, as they didn't own the Curtain. The brothers came up with a solution. They offered five of the Lord Chamberlain's Men the chance to become part-owners of a new theatre, for £10 each. They took up the offer.

In 1598, using this money, they leased land on Bankside, near the Rose. Now all they needed was a theatre – and they had one. Their lease with Allen said they owned anything built on the land. They took down the Theatre while Allen was away, despite protests from Allen's friends. Their builder stored it until it could be re-built on the Bankside site. Allen sued, demanding the building back. He argued the lease had run out, so the part about the building was no longer valid. He said it was his building. The case dragged on and went from court to court. Meanwhile the Theatre timbers became part of the new theatre on Bankside – the Globe.

A roaring success

The new theatre opened in 1599. It was a huge success. Many of Shakespeare's plays were performed there for the first time, including *Julius Caesar, Hamlet, Othello, King Lear*, and *Macbeth*. It could hold about 3,000 people when full – which it almost always was on public holidays and for the first day of a new play. The rest of the time, it was probably half to a third full. Then disaster struck.

Richard Burbage and the Lord Chamberlain's Men had been struggling for money when they built the Globe. They had roofed it with thatch, not tile, because thatch was cheaper. On 29 June 1613, at a performance of Shakespeare's *Henry VIII*, several small cannon were fired. They didn't use cannon balls, but they did use gunpowder held down with **wadding**. A piece of burning wadding caught in the thatch, which was soon alight.

Amazingly, no one was hurt. One man's **breeches** caught fire. Luckily, someone put those flames out with a bottle of beer, but the theatre burned down. It was big news. By the next day there were already two different songs printed about the event!

I was there...

Watching the Globe burn

The burning of the Globe was even mentioned in letters to friends! Here is part of a letter written by John Chamberlaine, a gentleman who lived on the other side of the Thames almost opposite the Globe, to his friend Ralph Winwood on 8 July 1613.

The burning of the Globe, or playhouse, on Bankside, on St Peter's Day fell out by a peal of chambers [firing of cannon]. The stopple of one of them landed in the thatch that covered it, burned it down to the ground in less than two hour, with a house next door. It was a great marvel, by the grace of God, that the people had so little harm, with only two narrow doors to get out.

The second Globe

By the time the Globe burned down, the Lord Chamberlain's Men were much better off. They were now called the King's Men, having been re-licensed after Elizabeth I died and James I became king. In 1609, they got a licence to play in the Blackfriars theatre that James Burbage had built. From then on, they played in the Globe in the summer and the Blackfriars in the winter rather than playing in the Globe all year round. Shakespeare's plays were still regularly performed, but he wrote no new plays for the second Globe.

The second Globe was built on the foundations of the first, so it was the same size and shape. But it was far more extravagant. They spent £1,400 on it. This compares to the Theatre which was valued at £700 during the court case with Allen in 1599. It opened in June 1614 and John Chamberlaine wrote to his sister, "I hear much speech of this new playhouse, which is said to be the fairest that was ever in England." It had a tiled roof, not a thatched one. The King's Men continued playing at the new Globe and the Blackfriars until the theatres were closed down by the government in 1642.

The third Globe

Now there is a modern Globe. It is as close as possible to the other two, but nearer to the river. It is a reproduction of the first Globe of 1599, not the second. So it is thatched, not tiled. The Shakespeare's Globe Trust wanted to recreate the theatre where most of Shakespeare's plays were first performed. They did huge amounts of research to make the theatre as accurate a reproduction as possible.

SHAKESPEARE'S EXPERIENCE

When did Shakespeare leave the Globe?

It is not known exactly when Shakespeare left the Globe, or London. This is what is known:
- He had been using the money he made to buy up land in Stratford, where many of his family still lived.
- His playwriting slowed down from about three a year at the start of his career to one a year towards the end of it. His last three known plays (written in 1613–1614) were **collaborations**.
- He died in Stratford in 1616, aged 52.

WHAT NOW?

New building, old techniques

The modern Globe was built, as far as possible, using the same methods as builders in Shakespeare's time. The builders, McCurdy and Co, prepared the timbers using the same techniques as used in Shakespeare's time.

This photo of the modern Globe was taken from the air in 2000.

How do we know?

How do we know what outdoor theatres looked like? The evidence is patchy and some of it is contradictory. Ideas change as new archaeological evidence is uncovered, such as the discovery of the site of the Curtain in 2012, or new documents are found or looked at again.

Archaeology

London has been rebuilt many times since Shakespeare's time. Archaeologists can only work if sites are uncovered, and most of the original Globe is under protected building. Archaeologists have investigated a small part of the Globe which is under a car park, and part of the Rose, across the street. These excavations provided valuable evidence about what the theatres were made of and even who went there.

Visual evidence

In Shakespeare's time, panoramas (bird's eye views), especially of cities, were popular. There are several panoramas of London from south of the River Thames that show the theatres. However, there are several problems with the accuracy of these. Some artists came to London, such as Wencelaus Hollar in 1607, but many others copied existing panoramas. As some were copying copies, it was easy at each stage for errors to creep in.

Official documents

Leases and contracts for building work give information about the size and shape of the buildings and how they were constructed. But they don't tell us everything. For example, the 1599 contract for the Fortune theatre has useful information, but also says "as at the Globe" or "bigger than the Globe" a lot. The Fortune's builder, Peter Streete, built the first Globe, so he knew those things. The Globe contract hasn't survived.

Theatre goers and the plays themselves

Theatre goers of all kinds have left descriptions and even drawings of their experiences. Letters, such as those of John Chamberlaine (see page 25), also give helpful details. While plays from the time do not have huge amounts of stage directions, there are enough for us to understand that there needed to be more than one doorway at the back of the stage for various entrances and exits. Many plays also need a central opening at the back of the stage, so it is reasonable to assume they had one.

I was there...

de Witt's London diary

This is a modernized extract from the diary entry written by Johannes de Witt, a Dutchman who visited London in 1596. A copy of his sketch of the Swan is below.

There are four amphitheatres in London so beautiful that they are worth a visit. In each of them a different play is daily offered to the public. The two more magnificent of these are situated to the south of the Thames, towards the South, and they are called the Rose and the Swan from their signboards... The largest and most magnificent of these is the Swan, as it holds 3,000 people.

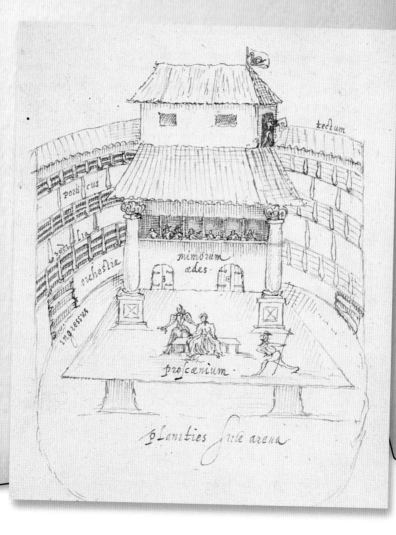

Indoor theatres

Public indoor theatres were smaller than outdoor theatres. They were very like private theatres and temporary theatres set up in large halls for private performances for nobles or for the court. However, these were open to the public and charged people to go in.

Shared features
All indoor theatres had:
- a roof – they were built inside an existing structure, usually on the first floor
- a large room
- seating on three sides
- a stage
- a backstage area, with doors to come onto the stage
- lighting by candles, as well as daylight through the windows.

A different experience
The use of candles meant, among other things, that there had to be short intervals while people replaced candles or trimmed the wicks to stop them smoking. Outdoor theatres had no interval, and the plays ran straight through. The lighting, and the smaller size of an indoor theatre, made it a different theatre-going experience. The seating included a limited number of seats on the stage. These, along with the boxes at the side of the stage, were the equivalent of the lords' rooms in outdoor theatres. You went there to be seen.

A different audience
The cost of going to an indoor theatre ranged from 6d to 2s and 6d. This meant that the audience was wealthier and, supposedly, more **cultured**. People once thought that very different plays were performed – with more speeches, more educated references, and less action. This may have been true, but by the time the Lord Chamberlain's Men were using the Globe and the Blackfriars, summer and winter, they did transfer some popular plays from the Globe to the Blackfriars.

WHAT NOW?

Two reconstructed theatres

The Shakespeare's Globe Trust always planned to build an indoor theatre, of the sort Shakespeare would recognize, in the building next to the modern Globe. A shell for it was built from the start. After much research and fundraising, further building work started in 2012. As with the modern Globe, the builders of the timber frame (McCurdy and Co again) used building techniques from Shakespeare's time as much as possible. The Trust uses the theatres as Shakespeare's company would have, playing in the Globe in summer and in the indoor theatre, the Sam Wanamaker Playhouse, in winter.

This is a digital image of the design of the 350-seater Sam Wanamaker Playhouse, which opened in January 2014.

How do we know?

What do we know about the Blackfriars theatre, where Shakespeare's company played in the winter from 1609? We have no archaeological evidence, but there are official documents that help us to understand the arguments that went on over adult companies playing there.

Why Blackfriars?

The Blackfriars monastery covered about five acres. This was a great deal of land. Because it was church land, it was a "liberty" – outside the control of the Lord Mayor and the Council. When the monastery was shut down, in 1538, the government left the land as a liberty. This made it very attractive to people who wanted land in the City free from Council interference. Much of the Blackfriars precinct was leased out to rich, important people, some of whom leased part (or all) of their share to other people. Who had leased what from whom and for how long became very complicated. Most of the story is known through the records of all the legal arguments.

SHAKESPEARE'S EXPERIENCE

Shakespeare and indoor theatres

Some of Shakespeare's plays were specifically written for indoor theatres, including *The Tempest*, *Cymbeline*, and *The Winter's Tale*. There is evidence that Shakespeare had experience of acting at court and for nobles. Many of his plays were performed at court, in indoor spaces, so he knew what to do differently. These spaces had a smaller stage, with audience members sitting on stage, which meant that plays with big battle scenes were a problem to perform. Even swordfights (although we know *Hamlet* played there) needed the actors to be quite cautious. On the other hand, the magic that was supposed to take place in *The Tempest* was probably even more magical by candlelight.

The first Blackfriars

In 1576, a boys company began to give public performances once a week in a large room in the Blackfriars precinct. They played, despite opposition from people in the precinct, until 1584 when their lease ran out. It was not renewed. In 1596, James Burbage bought a building inside the precinct for £600 and built an indoor theatre in it. He was refused a licence to play there, after complaints that it would be too disruptive. In 1600, the Burbages leased it out to another boys company. In 1609, the King's Men finally got a licence to play in the Blackfriars theatre and played there until the theatres were closed in 1642.

This is a reconstruction of an indoor theatre in the American Shakespeare Center in Staunton, Virginia, USA. It is taken from one side of the back of the stage, which has a door on either side of the stage and a large curtained entrance in the middle. There is a balcony above the stage, too, at the level of the higher gallery.

Who ran the theatres?

Most theatres had an owner, an acting company, and people hired by the actors. The company bought their plays from **playwrights**, although some owners directly bought plays. From 1581, a government official (the **Master of Revels**) was supposed to control everything by using licences. A licence was needed for a theatre, and to put on performances. The acting company needed a licence, too, as did the play itself. The government tried to control theatres and acting companies in this way. However, there is evidence that acting companies did play without licences and that theatres carried on even when told to close. The Curtain did this in 1600.

The theatre owner

Theatre owners were businessmen looking for a profit. Some had acting experience (James Burbage); some had run other businesses (Philip Henslowe). An owner first leased some land, preferably in the "liberties". Then he hired a builder to build his theatre. The cost varied. The Theatre cost £700 to build in 1576. As we have seen, the Globe cost £1,400 to rebuild in 1614. These were significant amounts of money.

The owner usually got a share of the takings from all performances, as rent. Burbage and Henslowe were the most successful owners. It helped that, for some years after 1594, Burbage's Theatre and Henslowe's Rose were the only **licensed** theatres. There were also occasional, unlicensed, performances at the Swan and the Curtain. Documents of Henslowe's that have survived show that between 1592 and 1597 he made about £360 a year. He had to pay for repairs and the licence fee (£1 to £3 a month in the period).

WHAT NOW?

Acting companies today
London acting companies are different now. Some companies, such as Propeller, stay together as a company, year after year. But many theatres, such as the National Theatre, build up the cast they want for each play. This means that many actors move around from show to show and theatre to theatre.

This is a painting of the actor Richard Burbage, a sharer in the Lord Chamberlain's Men after his father died. Some people think it is a self-portrait. It was certainly painted at the time.

Henslowe had to pay the "gatherers" who took the money. Some owners, such as Henslowe, also provided **props** and costumes. Owners probably made money from the food and drink sold in the theatre or near by. They sold it or let someone do so for a fee.

The acting company

An acting company leased a theatre from the owner. Until 1594, most owners rented for only two or three years. In 1594, the government licensed two companies (the Lord Chamberlain's Men and the Lord Admiral's Men) to use the two licensed theatres. After 1600, more companies and theatres were licensed. Most companies did not pay rent. Instead, they gave the owner a share of the takings, usually half.

Sharers

The acting company usually had about 10 sharers, made up of the most important actors. Sharers contributed to the costs of the company (usually the costumes and play books) and shared the profits. They signed agreements saying how long they would play together, what costs they would share, and how they would divide the profits. Some agreements also had other rules, such as not wearing costumes outside the theatre, and fines for arriving late or being drunk. Usually one of the sharers ran the company – sometimes giving up acting to do so. Sharers usually hired the rest of the company: minor actors, boys, and musicians. These people were paid a weekly wage, but no share of the takings.

Housekeepers

In 1598, the Burbages introduced "housekeepers": sharers who became part-owners of the theatres (see page 24). They shared the owner's expenses and takings. Company sharers had to sell their share back to the company if they left, usually for about £50. Housekeepers kept their share in a theatre and could pass it on in their wills when they died.

SHAKESPEARE'S EXPERIENCE

Shakespeare's work and sharing

Shakespeare was both a sharer in the Lord Chamberlain's Men and a housekeeper in the Globe. He was probably asked to be a housekeeper in order to tie him closely to the theatre and keep him loyal to it. Shakespeare probably made at least £200 a year from a combination of his sharer and housekeeper holdings, unless the theatres were closed for a long time by plague. The house he bought in Stratford was valued in documentation at £60. However, it was bought under a court system where it benefited the buyer and the seller to under-value the house, so it probably cost far more. He also bought farmland near Stratford worth £320 and a house in Stratford near his own, probably to rent out.

Edward Alleyn

Edward Alleyn is an example of how an actor can become a powerful figure in the theatre. He first appears as a 16-year-old actor with the Earl of Worcester's Men, in 1583. By 1589, Alleyn was in the Lord Admiral's Men, where he became the leading actor. In 1592, he married Joan Woodward, Philip Henslowe's stepdaughter. Alleyn was a famous actor. It was said he could make even a bad play watchable. While still acting, he also worked with Henslowe as a businessman. In 1600, they built the Fortune theatre and the Lord Admiral's Men moved there, with Alleyn as both owner and leading man. When Henslowe died in 1616, Alleyn inherited the businesses they had run together. He retired sometime between the years 1603–1606. Alleyn had enough money to buy the manor of Dulwich for £35,000 and to pay for a college to be built. He did not need to work again for the rest of his life.

This 1596 painting shows Joan Alleyn, dressed in her best. It is clear from her rich clothing that even before he was 30, her husband was doing well for himself.

What was it like to be an actor?

Only boys and men could become actors. It wasn't a respectable job, especially when theatres were first built. Well-off citizens and yeomen would not want their sons to become actors. There were two kinds of acting companies: the boys companies and the companies of both men and boys. Before 1583, when she set up the Queen's Men, Elizabeth I had preferred boys companies to perform at court.

Boys companies

Boys companies began to perform for the public in indoor theatres in 1576. They never used outdoor theatres, as their voices were more suited to a smaller theatre. Boys companies grew out of choir schools which performed at court and lived with a Master. They performed two or three times a week.

Adult companies

By the 1590s, there was a system of training. Boys joined a company at between 10 and 15 and were taught their trade by a particular actor. After a few years, they began paid work as hired men, then joined a company more permanently. Some moved around companies, but actors in Shakespeare's company tended to stay. Richard Robinson started as a boy, taught by Richard Burbage. He became a sharer and trained new actors. Each sharer signed a contract to stay for two or three years. Boys and young men played most female roles. Older female roles, especially the comic ones (such as the Nurse in *Romeo and Juliet* or Maria in *Twelfth Night*) were probably played by older men.

Fame and fortune

As theatres became more established, some actors became well known and could pull in an audience, no matter what the play. Among the most famous were the clown Richard Tarlton (and his dog, which was almost as famous), Richard Burbage, Edward Alleyn, and Nathan Field. Most of them didn't make more money than the other actors, although their popularity meant they were likely to become sharers.

WHAT NOW?

Playing a woman

Paul Chahidi played Maria in *Twelfth Night* at the modern Globe in 2002 and 2012. He was interviewed at the time:

> *I don't want it to be an impersonation of a woman or a drag act or something. People will either believe I'm a woman or not, and it won't be because I plucked every hair out of my body, it will be because I played a character truthfully, with strong and clear intentions. They'll know I'm a man, but you work with the audience at the Globe: we're all going to make an imaginative leap.*

These two male actors played female parts in *Richard III* at the Globe in 2012. You can see from the audience's faces that they, like Shakespeare's audience, have forgotten whether the actors are men or women, and are caught up in the characters' dilemma.

What did an actor earn?

Actors' earnings varied. Actors hired by a company could earn up to 10s a week in London, 5s when travelling. This might add up to £20 a year if the theatres weren't closed too often. It was about the same as a well-paid schoolteacher, but a schoolteacher would get free accommodation. Companies could have as many as 30 hired actors, but this was exceptional. Money was saved by "doubling" – one actor playing several parts. Boys learning their trade were paid anything from just their food and accommodation to 3s a week. These wage examples are from the Lord Admirals's Men, one of the most profitable companies.

Once an actor was a sharer (see page 36), he had a share in half of each week's takings instead of wages (about £50 in a good year). He also got a share of payments for private performances. One court performance could earn £7 to £10, plus a gift if the monarch enjoyed it. Some actors saved their earnings, often buying property. Shakespeare bought land and a house back in Stratford with his savings. Others didn't. Philip Henslowe's accounts show he often lent actors money.

Borrowing from the company

Here are examples of loans to actors (not for company business) from Henslowe's accounts:

12 December 1597:	lent to William Bourne, £1
6 April 1598:	lent to Humphrey Jeffes, £1
5 September 1598:	lent to Humphrey Jeffes to buy a pair of silk stockings, 15s
2 June 1599:	lent to Richard Jones, player, £5, to be repaid at 10s a week

Kidnapped!

Young actors with good voices were in demand. In 1597, Nathanial Giles was given permission to "poach" children from other schools and church choirs, for the Children of the Revels boys company that played at the Blackfriars indoor theatre. This meant he would get the best to play for the Queen, in the same way that the Master of the Revels had taken the best adult actors to form the Queen's Men in 1583. In 1602, Henry Clifton took Giles to court saying Giles had taken his 13-year-old son, Thomas, and seven other boys from their schools and had brought them to "a company of lewd and dissolute mercenary players" and forced Thomas to learn a part. When his father came to get him, Giles refused to give Thomas up, saying that his licence gave him power to take "any nobleman's son in the land". Clifton got his son back, but two of the boys taken at the same time thrived in the theatre. One of them, Nathan Field, went on to act and write plays for the King's Men.

Nathan Field was born in 1587. He was the son of a **Puritan** preacher, who would not have approved of actors and acting. He moved from a boys company to the Lady Elizabeth's Men in 1611, and then to the King's Men in 1616. Some people think he may have joined the King's Men to replace Shakespeare as a sharer.

Actors on tour

Successful London companies made more money in London than on tour. But even the most successful toured when the theatres were closed. The Queen's Men mainly toured and performed at court. The company that had the monarch as a patron was much more likely to get permission to play at the places on tour. In 1593–1594, when the theatres were closed for the plague, almost everyone was on tour. Tours made less money than theatre performances for several reasons.

- Travelling cost more. They had to pay for food, drink, and accommodation.
- Travelling took time. A man on horseback could cover about 48 kilometres a day. Touring players with a cartful of possessions would take longer.
- The audiences were much smaller. Sometimes the mayor and council allowed companies to play and paid them from the local government funds. They often said that the payment meant the company couldn't ask the crowd for money. Others allowed "a gathering", but the audience could still just wander off without giving anything.
- The mayor and council might give them permission to play, but not pay them, feed them, or find them somewhere to sleep.
- The mayor and council might refuse them permission to play, for various reasons. Some councils preferred to use the local, regular, acting company of the local noble.

I was there...

Repairs after a play

Here are just a few "costs" to local councils caused by players on tour. They often attracted large crowds, which could become unruly. The players themselves were not always very careful, either!

Canterbury, 1574: for candles and torches
Bristol, 1581: to mend the benches broken by the "disorderly" crowd
Barnstaple, 1593: to mend the Guildhall ceiling "broken by the players"
Exeter, 1604: for the scaffold [temporary stage]
Leicester, 1605: mending the chair in the parlour broken by the players
Leicester, 1608: mending the windows broken by the players (they left some money for this, but not enough).

This map shows places visited regularly by licensed touring companies, 1550–1642. As you can see, the whole of England was covered by one company or another.

Key
● Private homes
● Towns/cities

Edinburgh
SCOTLAND
North Sea
Newcastle upon Tyne
Irish Sea
Skipton Castle ●
York
ENGLAND
to Dublin
Chester
Tickhill Hall
Belvoir Castle
Shrewsbury
Leicester
Norwich
WALES
Hereford
Cambridge
Oxford
● Ingatestone Hall
Bristol
London
Canterbury
Barnstaple
Wilton ●
Southampton
Exeter
English Channel

Touring routine

Travelling companies were seldom more than ten men, and often were as few as six. Bigger companies (the largest was 20) might split into groups, or some actors might not tour. Actors got into costume outside a town. They entered the town banging a drum and singing, or calling out about the play. They marched to the Mayor's house, showed him their licence, and asked permission to play. Sometimes, for example if they feared the plague, the council might pay a company to go away.

Town councils might give acting companies permission to play in the town square, a large hall, or even a church or churchyard. They might pay them anything from 1s to £3 depending on the wealth of the council and the quality of the actors. If not, they usually gave the actors permission to go around the crowd, collecting money. The actors divided their takings daily or weekly and saved very little. In the winter of 1592–1593, Pembroke's Men, led by Richard Burbage, did so badly that they had to sell everything to get home. Their costumes fetched £80.

Touring abroad

Some acting companies went on tour to other countries. Some actors toured overseas regularly. Robert Browne first went abroad in 1590 to Leiden, in the Netherlands, with the Earl of Oxford's Men. In February 1592, he and three other actors went back there. They stayed in Europe while the theatres were closed (1592–1593), moving on to Germany. Several English companies toured northern Europe that year. When the company broke up in August 1594, one of them, Thomas Sackfield, stayed in Germany. It was possible to make about £60 a year there, more than twice as much as an ordinary actor would earn in England. By 1608, he was settled there, a rich man. Browne's family died of the plague and, apart from a brief return to England 1608–1612, he spent most of his time touring in Germany.

This 1650 painting of a town festival in the Netherlands shows a performance going on. The Netherlands was especially welcoming to English actors, having no professional companies of their own. After the theatres in England were closed in 1642, travelling in other countries was the only way for actors to work.

Missing home

Actors with families had to leave them behind when they went on tour. While touring the towns was not very profitable, those companies who managed to play in private homes could make a reasonable amount of money.

I was there...

A letter home

This is a modernized extract from a letter written by Edward Alleyn to his wife Joan, while he was on tour in 1593.

My good sweet Mouse,

Though the sickness [the plague] be round about you yet by God's mercy I pray it might escape your house. Make sure to keep the house clean and throw water out of the front and back doors each night. Put herbs up at the windows and pray. I have no news but that we are all well.

PS Mouse, you send me no news of anything, you should send of such things as happen at home, anything you like.

PPS I pray you let my orange woollen stockings be dyed black for when I get back.

WHAT NOW?

Keeping in touch today

Dickon Tyrrell played Hamlet's father's ghost and his uncle in the Globe's *Hamlet* in 2012. They toured the UK and then went to the United States for three months.

Three months is a very long time to be away from home. We survived mostly on Skype. You can do eye contact and read each other's faces, so you can see how someone is feeling. We Skyped twice a day and that made me feel much more in touch with all the little details of family life that I was missing out on. Because that's the thing, family life goes on without you when you're not there.

Writing plays

We don't know exactly when Shakespeare arrived in London, which company he joined, or when he began to write plays. We do know he was acting and writing plays by 1592. After the 1594 reorganization of companies and theatres, he was with the Lord Chamberlain's Men (later the King's Men), at the Globe and after 1609, at the Blackfriars.

Who wrote plays?

To be able to write plays, playwrights would have had some education. Many playwrights in Shakespeare's time had been to university, or the Inns of Court (which taught law). But some, like Ben Jonson and Shakespeare, hadn't. They seem to have had a **grammar school** education, joined companies, and learned on the job. Some people think companies had a new playwright work with an experienced one, as a sort of apprentice. Companies treated new plays as something to cut or add to, as needed. They were often written by several people, out of order. Sometimes they even used a plot by someone else.

Making money

New plays were in demand, but playwrights weren't paid well. The average payment for a play in the 1590s was £6. By 1614, the price was higher, but didn't reach £10 until the 1630s. Henslowe's accounts show how he worked with playwrights. Most companies (which usually bought the plays) probably worked this way. He asked for, or was offered, a play and gave a first payment. Sometimes he wanted playwrights to collaborate on a play. One might write the funny bits, one the tragic bits, and so on. Once written, the play belonged to the company. They could do what they liked with it. It had to be licensed by the Master of the Revels. The copy of the play he signed to show it was licensed was the valuable copy.

Henslowe's accounts are useful for finding out about playwrights, but only those who wrote for him and the Admiral's Men. So we can't find out about Shakespeare from them. However, they do make it clear that some professional playwrights made so little money (or were so careless with it) that they were in and out of prison for debt. Henslowe often bailed them out of prison, often on the promise of receiving a new play.

The 1998 film *Shakespeare in Love* shows Shakespeare writing alone and tossing aside sheet after sheet of barely used paper as he worked towards the perfect line. In fact, he collaborated in about 20 per cent of his plays and would have been more careful with paper. It cost about 1d for 10 sheets. An average play was 30 sheets long.

WHAT NOW?
Changing Shakespeare
Some modern actors and directors feel free to change Shakespeare's plays. They know that people know the stories of the most famous plays and that many people in an audience are reciting the most famous speeches in their heads. They cut them, they add new lines and even new characters. By doing this, they hope to make the plays seem fresh or to provoke discussion. Others treat Shakespeare's plays with a good deal of respect. If there are several versions of a play, they will consider them all before choosing one. They think carefully before cutting text. They think even harder before adding any text to one of Shakespeare's plays.

Collaboration

Playwrights often collaborated. It made them more productive, like a factory production line. Sometimes a group were paid as a team from the start. Sometimes one playwright took the first payment, but later payments were made to several men. Henslowe's accounts show that writing teams worked on several plays at once. This doesn't mean they sat and wrote together. They might have done, but it is more likely that they divided up the play and worked individually.

Teamwork

Henry Chettle, Robert Wilson, Thomas Dekker, and Michael Drayton often collaborated for Henslowe. Between 1 March and 31 August 1598, they wrote four plays together. They all also collaborated on several other plays. These were in smaller groups between themselves and with other playwrights. Sometimes a playwright wrote just one speech for a play or scenes with one character. Henslowe paid in at least two, or usually three, instalments. It took about a month from the first payment until Henslowe began to buy costumes or props for the play.

SHAKESPEARE'S EXPERIENCE

Shakespeare's collaborations

Shakespeare is known to have collaborated at the start of his career and at the end of it. People think Shakespeare probably collaborated on *Henry VI* (certainly Part 1, possibly Parts 2 and 3), *Titus Andronicus, Timon of Athens, Pericles, Two Noble Kinsmen, Henry VIII,* and *Cardenio* (a play that has not survived). He is thought to have written scenes and speeches for several other plays. There are about seven plays that are not in the First Folio (see page 50) that are thought to be mainly, if not completely, written by Shakespeare (see page 58).

This is a scene from the 2006 production of *Titus Andronicus* at the modern Globe. *Titus Andronicus* is one of the plays that Shakespeare is supposed to have collaborated on. It is full of action and conflict and almost everyone is dead by the end.

What did they write?

When Shakespeare started writing, it didn't matter if the story wasn't new. Playwrights took plots from history books, works by Roman authors, Italian stories, and even other English playwrights. What mattered was to tell the story well. Plays developed quickly in the 1580s and early 1590s, as did acting skills. "Personation" (writing or playing a believable character) became increasingly important. It was a skill Shakespeare certainly had as a playwright.

Playwrights wrote comedies, tragedies, and histories. There were funny moments in tragedies and dramatic moments in comedies. Most followed the tradition of **classical** plays: tragedies end in death and comedies end happily, usually with a wedding. The Master of the Revels **censored** all plays before giving them a licence. He took out political or religious references that might upset the government. Because of this, playwrights often set plays in imaginary or foreign countries so they didn't seem to criticize their government.

How plays changed

Plays changed to suit public taste. By the 1590s, plays referred to other plays or characters in them. There was a move away from romantic comedies towards **satirical** comedies about London. Shakespeare's company avoided these. Henslowe's didn't. One of their most popular plays was *The Shoemaker's Holiday* (1599), set in London. It made fun of people the audience would instantly recognize. Other playwrights then wrote "city comedies" set in London. Ben Jonson's *Every Man in His Humour* (1598) was set in an Italian city. He set it in London when the play was published in 1616.

Later, playwrights wrote more plays for indoor theatres. New plots became more popular than well-known stories. Plays avoided large-scale battles. They had more music and singing, less action, and more long speeches about ideas. Shakespeare's company followed this trend for their Blackfriars audiences.

What later became known as the First Folio was printed in 1623 by two members of Shakespeare's company, John Heminges and Henry Condell. It was the first published collection of Shakespeare's plays. "Folio" refers to the large page size. This copy of the First Folio was sold in London in 2006 for £2.5 million!

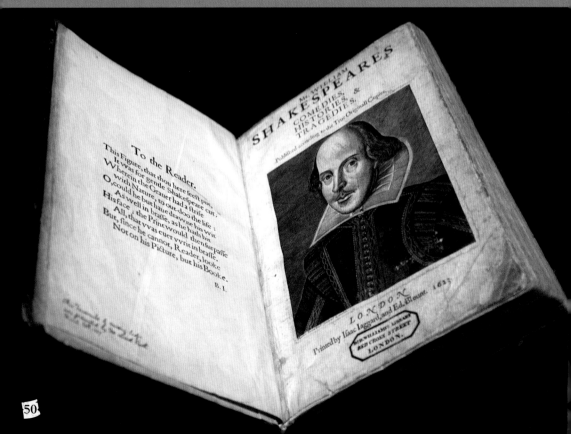

SHAKESPEARE'S EXPERIENCE

Greene's attack on Shakespeare

The year 1592 provides the first clear evidence for Shakespeare as a playwright and actor. Robert Greene, who wrote pamphlets and plays, died in 1592. A pamphlet was published that he had supposedly written on his deathbed. It was probably written by Henry Chettle, also a writer of pamphlets and plays. In part of the pamphlet, "Greene" urges three fellow playwrights to give up writing, because the profession is being taken over by the likes of Shakespeare. He tells them:

"There is an upstart Crow, beautified with our feathers, that, with his tiger's heart wrapped in a player's hide, supposes he is as well able to bombast out a blank verse as the best of you, and is, in his own conceit, the only Shakescene in the country."

Crows were seen as only able to copy other birds. He's suggesting Shakespeare is a fake who just copies them, who is also very vain and thinks he does it better.

Rivals!

Some playwrights wrote for one company, as Shakespeare did. Others, such as Ben Jonson, wrote for various companies. Playwrights were rivals, and they soon saw that playing up this rivalry amused people. Audiences felt "in the know" when comments about one playwright (or his play) were tossed into a new play or pamphlet. For example, Robert Greene attacked Shakespeare in 1592 (see panel). Shakespeare didn't retaliate, as far as we know. Later, there was a "war" between Jonson, John Marston, and Thomas Dekker in 1599–1601. It pulled in several other playwrights and drew good audiences. It is difficult to tell how serious these rivalries were. Some might have been deliberately started to gain public attention and big audiences.

How did you put on a play?

Putting on a play was different in Shakespeare's time. Companies didn't have directors as modern plays do. In Shakespeare's time, companies often performed a different play every day. Popular plays might be played more than once a week, especially when they were new. Modern plays run for weeks or months, even years, if very successful.

First steps

First, the company had to collect all the papers they needed. These were:

- the play, as passed by the Master of the Revels
- the "plot", the outline of the play, which hung backstage where everyone could see it before they went on
- a cast list
- a list of props for the prompter
- parts for each actor.

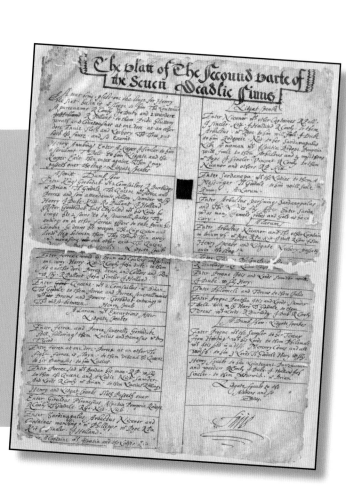

This backstage "plot" has survived from Shakespeare's time in Henslowe's papers. It is for *The Seven Deadly Sins*, a play from about 1590. It doesn't give the plot of the play. It lists the entrances and exits and what the actor should be taking on with him, such as a scroll.

Shakespeare's plays often had eight main parts, as the company had eight sharers. The parts were copied out by hand for each actor. They weren't given the whole text of the play, just their speeches along with the "cues" (the last words the actor speaking before him said). This saved time, money, and paper.

The company also needed all the scrolls used as props in the play (letters, official lists, and so on). The actors needed to remember to take these on. The words were not recorded anywhere else.

Rehearsal

Actors had short rehearsal periods for a new play. They were performing six afternoons a week and had to work on the plays they were performing, as well as on the new play. New plays probably had 18 morning rehearsals at most, although the actors might work some evenings and Sundays. Some plays went on with just a week of rehearsal. Audiences paid more to attend the first performance of a play. Even so, actors saw this performance as a rehearsal. It was their first chance to see how the play worked with an audience.

WHAT NOW?

Modern casts

Actors who perform in Shakespeare plays at the modern Globe rehearse for about six weeks. Most of the cast are in two plays in a season, with some overlap of the runs of the plays. They rehearse together – although not everyone is at every rehearsal when they begin. They don't rehearse on the Globe stage at first, but they use it several times before they perform to audiences. These are called "tech rehearsals".

The directors and the cast are changed each year, although some come back year after year. Auditions for the biggest parts are usually held several weeks before rehearsals start. All of Shakespeare's plays are in print, so the actors can get their own copies of the plays. They may well have seen the play before, in the theatre, or on film. They may even have studied the play at school, especially if it is one of the famous ones, such as *Macbeth* or *Romeo and Juliet*.

What were costumes like?

Companies wanted to create gorgeous effects as cheaply as possible. They focused on the main characters' costumes. Other actors wore their own clothes or re-used costumes the company owned already. Actors left each other clothes, some of which sound grand enough to be costumes, in their wills. If they could, the company re-used costumes for the main character. They changed the look by adding expensive lace, or a new cloak. Companies probably spent about £300 a year on costumes.

Henry Peacham made this sketch of a scene in *Titus Andronicus* in about 1595. Actors usually wore the fashion of the time, but this sketch shows they also tried for a "historical" look. The soldiers (far left) are in Elizabethan armour, but Titus (centre) and Aaron the Moor (far right) are in an attempt at Roman costume.

What about props and sets?

Just a few of the props listed by Henslowe in his accounts include: a rock, a cage, 3 tombs, 2 coffins, 1 bed, 2 steeples, 1 set of bells, 1 globe, 1 golden sceptre, 1 crown, 1 ghost's crown, 3 clubs, 17 fencing swords, 1 cupid's bow, 1 lion, 1 lion's skin, and the city of Rome. The idea that actors at the time performed on a bare stage with little in the way of props or scenery isn't quite accurate. Some companies couldn't afford much in the way of scenery or props and touring companies travelled with as little as possible. It would be more accurate to say that they were an added extra. Many plays have lines that help set the scene, without scenery, such as, "So this is the forest of Arden."

I was there...

Actors' costumes

In 1599, a Swiss tourist, Thomas Platter, wrote about his visit to London in his diary. He went to the theatre several times.

The actors are most expensively and elaborately dressed because in England important lords or knights leave almost the best of their clothes to their serving men in their wills. It is unseemly for the serving men to wear these clothes [it was illegal for servants to wear rich clothes], so they offer them for sale for a small sum of money to the actors.

Modern sets for Shakespeare plays can be very elaborate, unlike the sets of Shakespeare's time. Then, audiences were expected to exercise their imagination. This set, for *The Comedy of Errors* at the National Theatre in 2011, was very complicated. Each of the three buildings (right) rotated to provide a different set. The modern block of flats was behind and inside the centre building (below).

Special effects

Some stage effects in Shakespeare's time used the theatre itself. A stage bell sounded the time or rang alarms. Thunder came from beating drums, or rolling cannonballs along the floor of the space in the roof above the stage. Some theatres had a "thunder run", a rocking device with a cannonball in it. Lightning, on the other hand, needed fireworks. They were probably strung on lines from the heavens, going off one after the other starting at the top, so seeming to come from the sky.

Smaller effects

Murder and bloodshed were popular effects. A pig's bladder could conceal sheep's blood (which does not congeal) and guts for gory stage deaths. For less blood, they used a sponge soaked in ink, paint, or even vinegar. Companies had to be careful though – costumes were expensive and blood was hard to clean off. Body parts were made and used in many different plays. Henslowe's accounts list heads among the props.

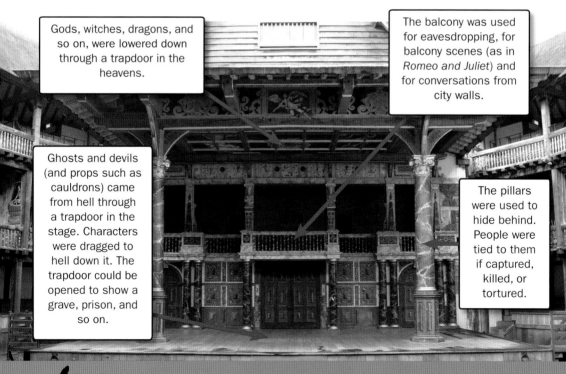

Gods, witches, dragons, and so on, were lowered down through a trapdoor in the heavens.

The balcony was used for eavesdropping, for balcony scenes (as in *Romeo and Juliet*) and for conversations from city walls.

Ghosts and devils (and props such as cauldrons) came from hell through a trapdoor in the stage. Characters were dragged to hell down it. The trapdoor could be opened to show a grave, prison, and so on.

The pillars were used to hide behind. People were tied to them if captured, killed, or tortured.

The Shakespearian stage had features that allowed for some big stage effects.

Make-up

Make-up was used in the theatre in various ways. A white face and red cheeks turned a boy into a beautiful young woman, as pale-skinned, fair women were seen as beautiful at the time. Used more heavily, white make-up showed a ghost or spirit. Black make-up was used for Moors with dark skin. Two characters with the same make-up (and, often, clothes) were twins.

Actors probably owned their own make-up. Henslowe's accounts show he did sometimes pay someone to do the actors' make-up, but they must have been able to do it for themselves as well, for touring.

SHAKESPEARE'S EXPERIENCE

Music and dance in Shakespeare's time

Music was an important part of performances in Shakespeare's time, especially in the indoor theatres, which had their own musicians. The boys companies had singing lessons and famous musicians wrote music for their performances. In outdoor theatres, trumpets and drums were for sound effects. The actors often made their own music, with stringed instruments, pipes, and a small drum. Up to at least 1600, outdoor theatre performances, even tragedies, usually ended with a jig – a dance by the clown of the company and some of the other actors.

Audiences enjoyed the jigs, as they seem to have enjoyed most of the various kinds of theatre performances at the time. While there were people who disapproved of the theatres, most who went had a good time. They threw themselves into the spirit of things. There must have been a big gap in London life when the theatres were closed in 1642, despite theatre-going having only been in existence for just over 70 years.

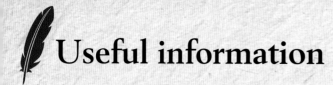

Useful information

Theatres in Shakespeare's London
This is a list of the theatres and when they were open in London up to 1615 while Shakespeare was living, working, or visiting there.

Outdoor theatres
Newington Butts opened 1576; used up to 1594 (not regularly)
Theatre opened 1576; used up to 1597
Curtain opened 1577; used beyond 1615
Rose opened 1587; used until 1606 (few performances after 1600)
Swan opened 1595; used until 1598 (then on and off, not each year)
Globe opened 1599; used until 1613 (burned down)
Second Globe opened 1614; used beyond 1615
Fortune opened 1600; used beyond 1615
Red Bull opened 1606; used beyond 1615
Hope opened 1614; used beyond 1615

Indoor theatres
St Paul's opened 1575; closed 1591; reopened 1599; used up to 1606
Blackfriars opened 1576; used up to 1584; reopened 1600; used by the King's Men (Shakespeare's adult company) from 1609; used beyond 1615
Whitefriars opened 1606; used until 1614
Porter's Hall opened 1615; used until 1617 (only used for a few performances)
Cockpit/Phoenix opened 1616; used beyond 1615

Shakespeare's plays
This list shows the plays that were mainly written by Shakespeare, in the order they may have been written in, with the possible date of writing. No one knows the exact order, or the exact date, in which they were written.
1590–1591 *The Two Gentlemen of Verona*
1590–1591 *The Taming of the Shrew*
1591 *Henry VI, Part II*
1591 *Henry VI, Part III*
1592 *The Two Noble Kinsmen* (by Shakespeare and John Fletcher)
1592 *Henry VI, Part I* (perhaps with Thomas Nashe)
1592 *Titus Andronicus* (perhaps with George Peele)

1592–1593 *Richard III*

1592–1593 *The Comedy of Errors*

1594–1595 *Love's Labour's Lost*

1595 *Richard II*

1595 *Romeo and Juliet*

1595 *A Midsummer Night's Dream*

1596 *King John*

1596–1597 *The Merchant of Venice*

1596–1597 *Henry IV, Part I*

1597–1598 *The Merry Wives of Windsor*

1597–1598 *Henry IV, Part II*

1598 *Much Ado About Nothing*

1598–1599 *Henry V*

1599 *Julius Caesar*

1599–1600 *As You Like It*

1600–1601 *Hamlet*

1600–1601 *Twelfth Night*

1602 *Troilus and Cressida*

1603 *Measure for Measure*

1603–1604 *Othello*

1604–1605 *All's Well That Ends Well*

1605 *Timon of Athens* (with Thomas Middleton)

1605–1606 *King Lear*

1606 *Macbeth*

1606 *Antony and Cleopatra*

1607 *Pericles* (with George Wilkins)

1608 *Coriolanus*

1609 *The Winter's Tale*

1610 *Cymbeline*

1611 *The Tempest*

1613 *Henry VIII* (by Shakespeare and John Fletcher; known in its own time as *All is True*)

1613 *Cardenio* (by Shakespeare and Fletcher; no known copy survives)

1613–1614 *The Two Noble Kinsmen* (by Shakespeare and Fletcher)

Wages in London in 1588

There were 12 pennies (d) in a shilling (s) and 20 shillings in a pound (£). The government set wages and they were the highest wage a person could be paid. Only the most skilful would have been paid this much. The amount is the yearly wage, assuming that the worker was also given food and drink.

Head brewer £10

Blacksmiths £6

Butchers £6

Weavers £5

Tailors £5

Hat maker £4 13s 6d

Baker £4 13s 6d

Knife makers £4 6s 8d

Shoemaker £4

Glover £3 6s 8d

Incomes

Various documents of the time give a very rough idea of the incomes of the nobility and gentry in about 1600.

Most nobleman would have an income (from rents) of about £3–5,000 a year (but the most important could have closer to £12,000).

Most knights would have an income (from rents) of about £1–2,000 a year (but the most important could have closer to £7,000).

Most gentlemen would have an income of about £500 a year (£1,000 for lands close to London).

Most yeomen would have an income of about £6.

The richest citizens, usually merchants, could have an income of about £10,000 in a good year, sometimes more.

Well-paid schoolteachers earned about £20 a year, with a rent-free house.

Prices

A loaf of bread 1d (size varies with the price of grain)

1lb (450g) of beef 3d

1lb (450g) of cheese 1d

1lb (450g) of soap 4d

A small pipeful of tobacco 3d

1 pair of workman's boots 1s

1 pair of citizen's fashionable boots 8s

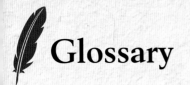

Glossary

apprentice someone who signs a contract to work for a master for a set number of years (usually seven) in order to learn a trade

arena open area surrounded by seating; used here to mean the baiting areas which had several levels of seating

baiting sport where an animal, usually a bull or a bear, is chained to a post so it can move around but not escape. It is then attacked by dogs.

breeches short trousers with the bottoms of the legs fastened just below, or just above the knee, depending on the fashion

burgess official or important citizen of a town

censor to suppress anything considered morally or politically unacceptable

character particular person in a play (such as the character of Juliet in *Romeo and Juliet*)

classical to do with the cultures of the "classical age" of ancient Greece and ancient Rome

clinker remains of burnt charcoal

cockfight a sport where two cocks (male chickens) are set to fight each other in a cockpit

collaboration something done with someone else

companies used here to mean groups of actors licensed by a nobleman

court the court was the king or queen and everyone who worked for him or her – servants, senior government officials, and so on

culture ideas, customs, and behaviour of a particular group of people or time

duties things that are expected of you

gentleman landowner with an income of over £500 a year, who has a coat-of-arms and the right to carry a sword

gentry social group made up of all gentlemen and their families

grammar school schools that were set up from the 14th century to teach Latin to young men (some also taught Greek and other subjects, such as music)

guildhall large room or building in a town where the town council met

household everyone, family and servants, who live and work in a particular house

income what a person earns

indoor theatre theatre inside a building, so not open to the sky

infamous well known for having a very bad reputation

inn place where travellers could buy food, drink, and a room for the night

lease pay a fee to use something. A document, also called a lease, is signed. It lays down the rules you have to follow, including when the lease ends.

liberties parts of London once owned by monasteries and not controlled by the City's laws

licence official piece of paper that gives you permission to do something

Master of Revels in Shakespeare's time, the person responsible for organizing the king or queen's entertainment. He also read plays and decided what could be performed or what changes had to be made before performances could take place.

nobility social group made up of all nobles and their families

nobleman from a family that is important in the country

official person who works for a government or large organization

pamphlet short booklet

petition request, usually asking someone powerful to do something for you

plague infectious disease, with a high death rate in Shakespeare's time. It had two forms: bubonic (worse in summer) and pneumonic (worse in winter).

play verb "to play" means to put on a play

playwright someone who writes plays

proclamation order made by the king or queen

prop movable objects used in a play, such as chairs, scrolls, plants, candlesticks, swords, and so on.

Puritan person who followed a strict Protestant religion

rights something the law allows people to dot

satirical mocking way of criticizing someone or something

tailor someone who makes clothes

vagrant homeless, jobless person, who moved from place to place looking for work

wadding small lump of soft material, used to keep something in place

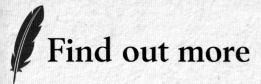

Find out more

Books

Shakespeare's Mousetrap, Margaret Frazer (kindle edition)

Shakespeare's Theatre, Andrew Langley (OUP, 2000)

Theatre and Entertainment (Shakespeare's World), Kathy Elgin (Cherrytree Books, 2005)

Websites

www.rsc.org.uk/explore/shakespeare
The Royal Shakespeare Company's website has lots of information about William Shakespeare.

www.shakespeare.org.uk/explore-shakespeare/about-shakespeare.html.
Find information about William Shakespeare on this website.

www.shakespearesglobe.com/about-us/history-of-the-globe
Learn more about the Globe on this site.

Places to visit

Where you can visit depends on where you live and what you can afford, but here are a few suggestions:

- If possible, visit a local reproduction theatre (see the map on page 43).
- Try to see a professional Shakespeare production. Think about where and when the director has chosen to set the production and how that affects your reaction to it.
- Go to see an amateur Shakespeare production. Some are very good and Shakespeare plays were meant to be performed, not read.

Suggestions for further research

Find out more about the evidence for outdoor theatres. On the following website, you can see a digital animation of the Theatre, the first theatre Shakespeare worked at.
www.museumoflondonarchaeology.org.uk/NewsProjects/Current-News/StepInsideTheTheatre.htm

Index